Keepi

Contents

	Page
Crossing the road	2-3
Riding in a car	4-5
Riding bikes or scooters	6-7
Swimming rules	8-9
Rules for the playground	10-11
Cooking rules	12-13
Rules for tools	14-15
Signs for safety	16

written by Pam Holden

1

You can cross a road after you look both ways.
Look one way, then look the other way, and then look back again.

2

Walk quickly across.
Don't run!
Go on a pedestrian crossing
if you can.

Put on your seat belt in a car.
Make it click.
Keep quiet so the driver can
hear sirens or horns.

4

Get out of the car on the safe side.
Keep away from the road.

Be careful on bikes.
Watch out for other riders.

Keep away from traffic.
Don't ride on busy roads.

Be a good swimmer.
Don't swim by yourself.
Wait for an adult to
look after you.

Watch other swimmers.
Don't go too deep.
Don't run near a pool.

Go to the playground
with an adult.
Watch out for swings.

Hold on when you go up high.

Work with an adult
when you cook.
Don't touch hot things.
They can burn!

Be careful if you use knives.

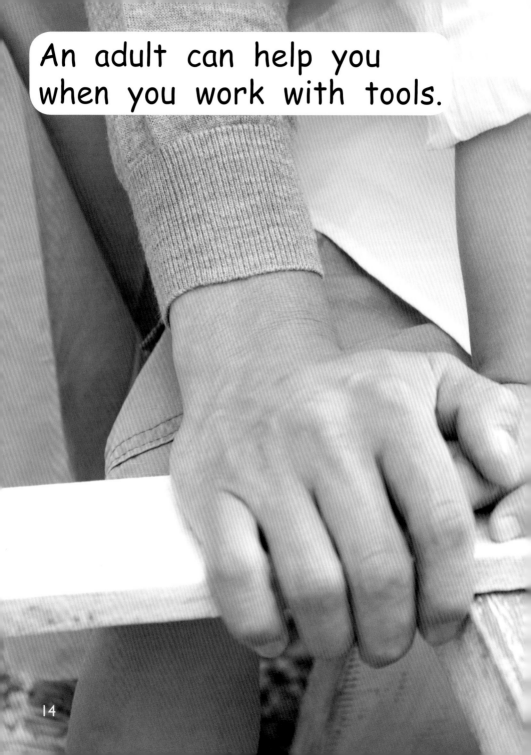

An adult can help you
when you work with tools.

14

A hammer can hurt!
Be careful with
sharp things, too!

Find out what safety signs say. Do you know how to get help fast?